NLP

— *DarkPsychology* —

The Secret Methods of Neuro-Linguistic Programming to Master Influence Over Anyone and Get What You Want

© Copyright 2018 by R.J. Anderson

All rights reserved.

The following Book is reproduced below with the goal of providing information that is as accurate and as reliable as possible. Regardless, purchasing this Book can be seen as consent to the fact that both the publisher and the author of this book are in no way experts on the topics discussed within, and that any recommendations or suggestions made herein are for entertainment purposes only. Professionals should be consulted as needed before undertaking any of the action endorsed herein.

This declaration is deemed fair and valid by both the American Bar Association and the Committee of Publishers Association and is legally binding throughout the United States.

Furthermore, the transmission, duplication or reproduction of any of the following work, including precise information, will be considered an illegal act, irrespective whether it is done electronically or in print. The legality extends to creating a secondary or tertiary copy of the work or a recorded copy and is only allowed with express written consent of the Publisher. All additional rights are reserved.

The information in the following pages is broadly considered to be a truthful and accurate account of facts, and as such any inattention, use or misuse of the information in question by the reader will render any resulting actions solely under their purview. There are no scenarios in which the publisher or the original author of this work can be in any fashion deemed liable for any hardship or damages that may befall them after undertaking information described herein.

Additionally, the information found on the following pages is intended for informational purposes only and should thus be considered, universal. As befitting its nature, the information presented is without assurance regarding its continued validity or interim quality. Trademarks that mentioned are done without written consent and can in no way be considered an endorsement from the trademark holder.

Table of Contents

Introduction 6

Chapter 1: The Background of Dark Psychology . 7

Chapter 2: The First Step — Understanding People 12

Chapter 3: Psychoanalyzing People 18

Chapter 4: Knowing Your Position 24

Chapter 5: A Favorable Position — Getting Yourself Ahead 28

Chapter 6: The Power of Words — Linguistic Foundations of Manipulation 32

    Spinning ideas 32

    Overselling as a tactic 34

    Oversimplifying 35

    Overt honesty... 35

    Define your position as neutral 38

    Intersperse long and short 40

    Intensity and passion 41

    Know your aura 42

    Spill yourself 43

    Play to your strengths.................................... 45

Avoid condescension 47

Be charming 48

Making the impossible possible 49

How to get the flakes 50

Know your contrarians 51

Strike people off-guard 53

Make them feel special 54

Recognize everything as a variable 55

Chapter 7: Language and Psychology — Words to Make People Tick 57

Chapter 8: Understanding Breaking Points 63

Chapter 9: The Art of Lying 66

Chapter 10: "I See Myself in You" — The Importance of Identification 73

Chapter 11: Navigating the Psyche — Predicting Reactions 77

Chapter 12: What to Do If You're Discovered — Regaining Favor 81

Conclusion 87

Thank you! 88

Introduction

Congratulations on purchasing *NLP* and thank you for doing so.

The following chapters will discuss how to use neuro-linguistic programming and dark psychology techniques to manipulate people and get everything that you want out of them. This is a wealth of information that I've built up over a lifetime. I can't tell you how you should use it. I can only say that, if used appropriately and cleverly, these are the tools you can use to get ahead of everyone else. Use this information with caution, because these are very real secrets of the human psyche, and they can easily be used to manipulate people.

There are plenty of books on this subject on the market, so thanks again for choosing this one. Every effort was made to ensure it is full of as much useful information as possible, please enjoy!

Chapter 1: The Background of Dark Psychology

This book explores neuro-linguistic programming, which is one major facet of dark psychology.

It's a bit of a well-kept secret that the ability to manipulate people is a useful tool. It's one of the reasons how businessmen and politicians get and hold their positions. There comes a certain point in your life wherein completely turning off your emotions and being pragmatic is a skill you need to have. Nobody likes to discuss it because we have this societal fear of the reality that people can just be seen as a means to an end.

The late Steve Jobs was particularly renowned for his ability to work people's emotions and to say just the right thing that would get them to come around to his view. It was so strong, in fact, that the people around him developed their own term for it: the 'reality distortion field,' a phrase coined from a similar phenomenon in the Star Trek universe.

There are numerous historical instances of Steve Jobs taking advantage of his unique ability to get precisely what he wanted. One such instance was when Jobs, in the 1980s, was trying to get Pepsi CEO John Sculley to come to Apple. This exchange spawned a famous line that many know today: "Do you want to sell sugared water for the rest of your life, or do you want to come with me and change the world?"

There is a lot that can be said about his specific ability to charm and manipulate people, not the least of which was his deep understanding of what people wanted as well as what people wanted to hear. Add on to this an understanding of subtle intimidation, power cues, and a large amount of passion and charisma, and you have a powerhouse who could get pretty much whatever he wanted.

How does all of this apply to you? Well, you're

reading this because you want to learn how to work with people from the inside out. You want to know how to say just the right thing to get what you need and how to manipulate people such that you can bypass any obstacles, so they will do exactly what you want. If that's the case, then you've come to the right place.

The fact is that the mind is a relatively simple thing. While the brain is infinitely complex, the manifestations of the conscious mind are both resolute and easy to work with. Most people work in very obvious and predictable ways such that if they're a 'normal' person, you can rather easily figure out the best way to work with them in no time flat.

The purpose of this book is to analyze all of these patterns within the context of people in general so that you can learn the best way to put these trends to use. Some people will, of course, break these 'standard' molds, and for this reason there are a couple chapters dedicated to the idea of knowing the person you're working with, reading their inner and outer body language and mental cues, and knowing how to build a paradigm that you can easily manipulate them with.

In the end, this book is about using the concept of neuro-linguistic programming to its fullest to get what you want out of people. A more common term for this is 'manipulation.' However, the aim of neuro-linguistic programming is slightly different. Neuro-linguistic programming is more focused on the long-term shifting of attitudes where manipulation is more based on immediate gains. That isn't to say that neuro-linguistic programming isn't a form of manipulation though, it absolutely is.

When you hear the term 'manipulation,' you will probably have some sort of knee-jerk reaction like, "Wait, isn't manipulation wrong?" And to this question, there is no simple answer.

I have to say no, though. Manipulation isn't wrong, manipulation is simply a tool. How you use it can determine whether it's wrong or not.

For example, an example of manipulation being objectively wrong is doing something that gets somebody terribly hurt. There are also some unspoken rules that you should never break. For example, while it's pretty easy to take advantage of the fact that somebody's parent is dying, actually doing *so* is a major ethical gray area.

If you stick to maintaining an ethical approach, then manipulation actually proves itself as a method of understanding people and knowing how to work with them so things will work out better for you. You can even use manipulation for good purposes. One such example is Steve Jobs yet again, who used his reality distortion field for good causes, such as when he would convince his employees that it was possible to do something that was more or less impossible, which in turn, would make them work harder for the end result and eventually lead to a new mark being set in technology.

In the end, it's your choice how you use the tools outlined in the book.

Chapter 2: The First Step — Understanding People

The first critical step to making people's emotions work for you is to build your understanding of people and why they work and react the way that they do. It's difficult to consolidate a lifetime of noticing these patterns into a simple book, but there are a lot of broad categories that we can cover.

Everybody has different things which make them the way they are. Really, everybody is just the culmination of their unique set of experiences which eventually brings about the development of a larger and cohesive image of a whole for the person. Because of this, there are often a great many avenues that you can pursue to get to know somebody better as a person at the most basic level.

It's at this point that I really need to drive home

the importance of knowing how to be attentive. The truth is that a lot of the things in this book require a very heavy understanding of how to read into people's subtleties. This is a skill that you will need to build if you want to become good at neuro-linguistic programming. People wear themselves rather loudly. If you can't read into these subtleties, then more or less you're just going to get lost.

People often have a few different traits which you can use to understand them. Things such as their body language, their life situation, and their emotions. All of these impact one another. In the following chapters, we will break down all of these aspects to help you understand exactly what position you're in.

Body language is a huge giveaway about what's going on in a person's head. Understand that in terms of neuro-linguistic programming, body language is a language in and of itself.

We're going to expand on this concept just a bit

so we can gain an understanding of how we can read and process other people's emotions.

This is actually a very critical part of neuro-linguistic programming, and one of the things that makes it such a challenge. Doing it properly is not like picking a lock. There is no 'correct' path for you to do it right. It's a very dynamic activity, which is heavily centered on your ability to understand what the other person is thinking in a very concrete manner.

Understand that a person has many physical tells, but that's not the be-all-end-all of what is going on in a person's mind. Some people are so good at hiding their emotions that you can't really tell what's going on under the hood unless you know them very well.

Often, people will have two emotions running in parallel. These can be difficult to decipher, but generally, they have the emotion at their foreground — this is what they display themselves to be feeling — and they have their emotion in the background, which is what they are feeling under the hood.

Some people are worse than others when it comes to hiding their emotions while some people make no effort at all. There are times, too, where these emotions may run in tandem and are exactly the same.

The truth is, though, that if you're trying to convince somebody of something, you always have to consider the possibility that people don't often feel what they're projecting themselves to be feeling. Usually, you have to consider what these parallel emotions could be.

We'll focus more on the underlying emotions when we get to the chapter on psychoanalysis. However, for now, we just need to focus primarily on reading emotions on the surface.

People convey a lot of their emotions through their body language as well as through their tone of voice and their choice of words.

If you pay attention to a person's eyes, you can read a lot into somebody's foreground emotion. While, hopefully, you're emotionally competent enough to read foreground emotions relatively well, note that some of these can be difficult to break apart from one another. For example, while the difference between annoyance and anger are slight in terms of their physical display, they have far different emotional connotations. Annoyance is much shorter and less severe, though perhaps more immediately snappy. Anger is more brooding and harder to work your way out of.

Their tone of voice will also tell you a lot. Often, when people aren't being completely honest about the emotion they're presenting, their voice will sound ever so slightly off. Being able to recognize this and using context clues to figure out what's really bothering them or going on in their head is very important.

Sometimes their choice of words will give you hints as well. Pay attention and try to notice if their sentences are structured differently. Are they shorter? Is their choice of words more serious than usual?

In essence, pay attention to a person's body language, as it will tell you a lot about what you need to know when it comes to what a person is feeling, at least on the surface level. When you combine that with your analysis of their underlying conditions, you actually get a very potent piece of information that you can work with.

Chapter 3: Psychoanalyzing People

In this chapter, we're going to expand our knowledge of foreground emotions that we covered in the last chapter and talk about going deeper into a person's psyche to figure out their background emotions.

This can be difficult in and of itself because people aren't always even aware that they're experiencing background emotions. Trying to break into them can be difficult in that case. In such a situation, you need to be more reliant on your knowledge of people in general as well as the person in question to see what's going on underneath it all.

Normally, people manifest background emotions in a couple of ways. There is immediate overcompensation, immediate under-compensation, and using a coping mechanism.

Immediate overcompensation is often used in the face of shocking emotions. There are a few tells when it comes to immediate overcompensation. Consider the case of somebody trying to stay strong when they hear bad news. Their immediate reaction is to maintain eye contact and force a smile and a 'happy' tone. However, if you focus more closely, there are obvious tells. Their eye contact, for example, will be eerie and a bit too strong, and they may purposefully attempt not to move their eyes to stop themselves from shedding tears. The smile will be clearly forced because it won't be present in their eyes, or they will show a neutral face that's too stiff and unaffected. On the inverse, the tone of their voice will be so affected to the point that they either sound robotic, or they sound like they're a waiter at a restaurant trying to get a tip.

Immediate under-compensation is the exact opposite problem. Instead of trying too hard to hide their secondary emotion, they may only partially try to hide it, leading to some pretty obvious tells. This is a lot less common than overcompensation, though, so it's not too important in a relative sense.

What's really important is to understand the development of coping mechanisms. The development of coping mechanisms is a central part of psychoanalyzing people, and learning how to undermine these and break inside of them — as well as understanding why they form in the first place — is a central component of manipulating people.

The development of coping mechanisms often occurs over a long period of time. It can be seen as a way of overcompensating in response to a given unwanted stimulus which occurred either once or many times.

One of the most prominent and easy to identify coping mechanisms is the development of a power complex. These normally develop because of a period in a person's life where all power and autonomy was stripped. Perhaps they grew up with narcissistic parents, for example, and were never allowed to make their own decisions. In response to this trauma, when they are older, they deal with the emotional strain by taking advantage of power whenever they can possibly get it.

When you recognize a power complex, you start to develop routes that you can use to manipulate these kinds of people. For example, you have two different kinds of approach you can use to handle someone with a power complex.

The first is the most obvious, appeal to it. If you work with the person in a way that you actually appeal to their power complex, you can get them to feel like they're in charge even if they aren't. This can be a useful tool, but there's a lot of things you need to consider before you can do it correctly. For example, you have to layer everything, so it seems like they really are in charge and not like you're just trying to get them to feel like they are. A cunning way of doing this is to put yourself 'under' them by lowering your tone of voice. Don't be defensive, but make yourself sound vulnerable by changing your tone of voice ever so slightly.

The second is a little bit strange, you can try to exert more control over them. This one is far more difficult to pull off than the last one. If somebody gets off on having as much power as possible, you can try to undermine their power by acting in a manner such that you're superior to them. In other words, emotionally emasculate them. You can do so by prodding at some of the things that you think bother them and use these things to get under their skin in a subtle way that they don't notice you doing it. The repercussions of this technique are much greater though. You can effectively change the dynamic so that you're in charge. However, you can also mess up terribly and make the other person angry enough to shut you out completely.

Being able to recognize a lot of these things and patterns is essential to manipulating people and getting a grasp on them through neuro-linguistic programming, so be sure to take time to study up on what kind of things people usually carry with them. A lot of them are pretty clear: poor childhoods, getting bullied in school, and so on and so forth.

Chapter 4: Knowing Your Position

Before you do anything else, it's important that you learn to recognize and work with your position. What is your position, exactly? Imagine your relations with this person in terms of a game board. You're attempting to get from one end to the other through a series of different interactions. At the other end of the board lies your end goal.

If you're fortunate, you can innately perceive somebody's warmth towards you. Their warmth to you will indicate how near to your end goal you are and how well you can manipulate them to get what you want. Remember that the end goal of all of this is whatever you want to get out of them. You're trying to say the right things and do the right actions so you can reach that goal.

It's at this point that you can start to roll all of the

stuff that we've talked about in the chapters prior into one big lesson to get a feeling of that person's level of intimacy towards you. It's actually surprisingly easy to build up intimacy. We'll be going over the techniques to accomplish this in the following chapter, actually.

How can you perceive how intimate somebody is with you? You can judge it as a function of their willingness to be open with you.

To influence people using neuro-linguistic programming, you need to garner favor with them. Garnering favor doesn't consist of doing favors and being on their feet all the time. Rather, it's the contrary. Almost everyone doesn't like people who are total kiss-ups and will be turned off by people who act in such a manner. The exception, of course, is people who have power complexes. However, in this case, they will largely exist for the benefit of the person with the power complex where they will be walked all over instead of garnering any real sort of influence.

The reality here is that there are a lot of ways that you can garner favors from somebody. Some of these will be discussed in more detail on in the following chapter. For now, we're just going to cover the basics.

The first thing that you need to realize as somebody who wants to influence others is that people will see their relation to you in a couple of different ways. The first is their emotional intimacy with you, the second is their trust in you, and the third is their expectation of you. All of these elements relate to each other, but they also diverge. You can build favor with somebody by increasing these three fundamental elements as much as possible.

Emotional intimacy is built through conversation. People like to be seen as people rather than being seen as some monolith, they want to be humanized. If you need something from somebody, don't treat them like they're special. Treat them as though they're your friends, and they will start to come around and act like they were your friends. Small things can go a long way in this instance.

On top of that, you need to start building their trust in you. This will naturally build over time as you work on the other two elements mentioned earlier. Trust here refers to their ability to trust your judgment than their ability to trust you as a person. In that respect, it can be seen as its own individual category. Therefore, when you're trying to gain somebody's trust, you're trying to gain their ability to take what you say at face value and not question it too much. People are naturally a bit skeptical when they're presented with an idea.

Chapter 5: A Favorable Position — Getting Yourself Ahead

In this chapter, we're going to talk about building a personality for yourself that will immediately allow you to become emotionally intimate with somebody and gain everything that you need to build a connection with them and successfully manipulate them.

Once you familiarize yourself with the methods discussed in this chapter, you'll be able to easily and efficiently garner the trust of people and use verbal and non-verbal communication to your advantage to get what you want out of them. In some cases, you only need to have a little conversation, though your abilities will become better as your rapport with people extends. Maximum effectiveness is reached after multiple conversations.

From there, you can start using the methods in

the next chapter to orient people towards a certain goal of yours. That is when the book really starts to pick up in terms of content. Everything up to this point has been simple in a relative sense. We'll get down to the nitty-gritty there.

Before we get to the point of influencing people, though, we need to talk about how you can put yourself in a position to influence these people. So what exactly can you do to put yourself in that sort of position?

The first and foremost thing that you want to focus on is your presentation to them. The way that you present something to somebody will tell them more or less everything about you, so a strong presentation is absolutely crucial. Note that the personality that you develop in this chapter should be an extension of your own rather than one from scratch. If you attempt to make one up from scratch, then it might come across as just contrived, which is the opposite of what you want.

Rather, you want to come across as genuine. Painfully so, in fact. It's at this point that you're going to realize that a lot of the things that you think are taboo in conversation aren't and that taking advantage of these things can be a great way to make somebody open up to you.

However, while you should be genuine, you should also do what you can to mirror them. Don't do so in an obvious way. However, research shows that people are more receptive to people that emulate their body language. Doing so without looking strange can be rather difficult in and of itself, but start small and then work your way up. If they have their face in their hand, then you should assume a common position. Make it look natural, not like you're specifically trying to mimic their body language. When you do mimic somebody's body language, you open up a new level of intimacy that wasn't there before. This is crucial in the pursuit of emotional connection to somebody, so make sure that you do this.

Do note, though, that there are times where you can assume power positions. These come after you've built rapport with somebody. Power positions are body poses which indicate that you're in control of the situation. They usually consist of taking up as much space as possible without looking obvious (for example, leaning back in a chair with your arms crossed), or otherwise being in some sort of position over somebody (e.g., standing when they're sitting). Subtle power plays like these can go a long way in establishing a dominant position over somebody, but they tend to take the subtlety out of your manipulation, and it can make people feel like they're being controlled, so use them sparingly.

With all of this said, we'll move on to discussing some of the ways that you can use your words to persuade people and get what you want.

Chapter 6: The Power of Words — Linguistic Foundations of Manipulation

In this chapter, we're going to cover how you can manipulate people in a conversation itself through the magic of neuro-linguistic programming. Specifically, we're going to talk about several different strategies that you can address in dealing with people to get what you want. The big goal here is the development of your very own 'reality distortion field.' There's a lot more to it than this, but it's a great starting point, and if you practice them, you'll quickly find yourself getting whatever you want. With that said, let's start.

Spinning ideas

The first thing you need to bear in mind before anything else is that when you present an idea to somebody, you'll find yourself pushing against the current because of the very nature of the proposition. This is because most of the time, you are not in the winning position in terms of influence. People don't really want to do something unless they have to, especially if it seems unreasonable from their end for one reason or another.

Because of this, one skill that you really need to work on is the spinning of different ideas so that they sound advantageous to the person you're trying to influence. You don't have to do this directly. In fact, you should avoid doing it as this will make your attempts obvious.

Rather, instead of presenting things in terms of 'you' and 'I,' present them as 'we' so that they see their inclusion in your plan. If you speak directly of benefits, then do so in a way that makes it sound like you both benefit from it, leaving out your potential benefits.

Overselling as a tactic

The reality is that if you want to influence people properly, you have to dream big. While people are apprehensive about things which are big and difficult, they are more likely to come around to things that are bigger than reasonable, provided that you can sell them as reasonable. The key here is to have passion in your presentation.

Realistically, you know internally that you aren't going to hit the mark if you go through with whatever you're trying to do. However, falling just short of the mark is completely acceptable. It also works reflexively, if the person you're influencing has enough respect for you and you don't do the overselling thing constantly, they may see themselves as the issue and be more responsive to the idea of doing something else for you.

Overselling is a risky tactic because you must have the ability to inspire people with your passion. However, through persistence, practice, and the development of the right charisma, you can easily get away with overselling to get what you want out of people.

Oversimplifying

The 'sunk cost fallacy' is a very real thing, and if somebody devotes themselves completely to something, there's a very low chance that they will want to get out of it. This is just the simple truth of the matter. You can easily make people sympathetic to your idea by simply making it sound small, and then you let them find out that it's bigger once they're already involved. People very seldom want to be the weak link in something.

This can be seen as the exact opposite of overselling. Instead of making it obvious how a project or something that you want will go, you can hide it and mention it later.

Overt honesty

This is one of the easiest tactics here, but it will

make people respect you more and make them more partial to your influence. The simple fact is that a lot of people aren't used to honesty when they least expect it. More than that, the way to influence people — to really and honestly influence people — is to throw them off. If you want to influence people, you have to bewilder them and overpower them in terms of willpower. Consider it like a boxing match, you wait for your opponent to give you an opening before you throw a punch. However, here, you can create your own openings. You can give yourself an opening by doing things that people don't ordinarily expect, and this can earn their respect.

Being honest when people don't expect it is a huge part of successfully implementing this technique. Of course, you need to have a good sense of timing. Don't tell people that something is horrible or that their outfit looks bad or anything else explicitly rude. Rather, if you feel like everybody else is coddling them about something, be the opposition to the coddling.

People know when they're being fed manure, even if it's just manure to make them feel better. Being somebody who sees through the manure will make them feel like you really understand them. We'll discuss more on when this is a good or bad idea when we get to the chapter regarding 'breaking points.'

It's hard to define exactly what overt honesty means. It's a bit of a tricky definition in and of itself, after all. If you really want a definition of overt honesty, consider a situation where somebody is confiding something in you. They're nervous about some big life decision that's coming up. Overt honesty is not directing them to take one path or another, even if that's your ultimate goal in the conversation. Overt honesty is like them saying, "I just hope it will be okay," and then saying something like "It might not. You know that, and I'm sorry you're in this situation. It's awful. But..." and then proceed to carry on the conversation, slowly trying to swing them to your side through the use of other tactics.

The key here is letting them recognize that you understand them. Most people on the other end of the conversation would tell them "It will absolutely be okay," but you don't do that. You affirm their underlying fear (that it might not be okay), validate that fear by expressing it back to them, and make them feel like they should allow you to help them make a decision, even if it's not in a direct manner. This makes them subconsciously take your advice to heart than they would the advice of others.

Define your position as neutral

This won't always apply, but there are some times where the best course of action is to explicitly define your position because it makes you seem like you're taken out of the situation. Even if you have a position that you want to push somebody towards.

Consider this, you and one of your friends have a mutual friend who you don't like to have around for one reason another. You and the mutual friend are talking to one another at a party after everybody else goes to sleep, and they start to confide in you that they have the opportunity to move eight hours away. (This story is based on something which actually happened to somebody close to me.)

Since they're only a mutual friend, you can say that you're in a unique position. "Everybody else will push you to stay because they're your friends and they'll miss you. I'm in a unique position because I know you, but it doesn't really make a huge difference to me if you're here or there. See what I'm saying? I like you, don't misunderstand. I want to be your friend. I consider myself your friend. But I'm in a unique position because I can tell you without bias what you should do. This is an incredible opportunity for you, and I think you should go."

Because you defined your neutral position and you've hopefully done other things in this list to put yourself in a position such that you can influence their position, you have subconsciously gotten them to start thinking that your opinion is the objective one and everybody else's is simply subjective. You are the beacon of rationality here. This one goes best with a little bit of drinking because it eases their suspension of disbelief.

Intersperse long and short

This goes really well with the last lesson, but it's a great tip in general. When you're talking to somebody, don't absolutely dominate the conversation. Allow them to talk and then ask relevant questions about what they're saying, tying it into your overarching point. This is more aimed at casual conversation than selling an idea, but you can also use it to sell an idea. (Keep your responses and questions short, but throw in an occasional passionate and long explanation.)

By interspersing long statements and short statements, you accomplish two things. The first is that you keep people on their toes in terms of what to expect from you in the conversation, which keeps them engaged. Also, when you respond to whatever they're saying, make it seem as though you genuinely care about whatever perspective they're sharing.

This is a very key part of influence, so be sure to use it when you can. Remember, you're trying to keep people on their toes and keep them interested, as well as to ultimately make a case for something whether directly or indirectly.

Intensity and passion

You need to work to make yourself intense and passionate or at least give other people the impression that you are. This is more geared towards pitching ideas than in casual conversation. If you do this in a casual conversation, you may actually stray off the path to successfully influencing somebody because you might come off as creepy.

What you can do instead is to work at making your sentences 'sharp.' Avoid saying filler words and practice saying exactly whatever it is that you want to say. The more you stumble around things, the less confident that you will seem.

Moreover, you can make yourself come off as more passionate if you just add more enthusiasm. It doesn't matter if you repeat the same information so long as you phrase it a different way, or you can even just make it sound like it's there for emphasis. The point is to develop a rhythm for whatever you're doing and sound genuinely excited about it. Make it sound like not only do you want it to happen, but you're one hundred percent confident that it can happen as long as you have the other person's help. This also goes hand in hand with some of the things we talked about earlier, like making them feel as if they're an important part of whatever you're suggesting.

Know your aura

Whether we like to admit it or not, everybody has a certain aura or vibe that they give off. Knowing what sort of aura or vibe that you give off is important to determine what kind of approach you should take to influence people.

Spill yourself

People often make themselves very vulnerable to other people. However, most of the time, they'll only do this as a reaction. If you'll be the first to make yourself 'vulnerable,' then you can often get them to open up as well. This can be a great way to learn how to get under their skin, as well as to learn what sort of tactics you need to use to influence them.

There are two different routes that you can take here. The first is people know about you. This has a few consequences but also a few perks. The most obvious consequence is that this opens you up to being emotionally vulnerable to the other person. If you can't shut your emotions off completely, then you may find yourself growing attached to them. This isn't good if you just want to use them for gaining something. On the other hand, depending on the stories that you shared, this might mean that people may corroborate with you if you ever need them. I would personally have a few stories on reserve that don't particularly matter if they get out, because if someone realizes that you're using them, they may get angry and retaliate by leaking your 'secrets' if they're immature.

The second route is that you can make up stories. This one is best done over the phone or in person rather than through email or text message. If you make up stories, then you can rest easy that they have no actual attachment to you in a real sense. You may even set up a reserve of fake stories for different situations. An added benefit of this method is that if they decide to leak your secrets, so long as you don't leave a paper trail, you can accuse them of making up things to defame you since nobody will be able to corroborate what they're saying about you. This also serves as the primary drawback, though. If you need somebody to corroborate your own story, you either have to go without it or let somebody know that you're trying to use somebody else, which can cause a bunch of problems in and of itself.

All in all, though, if you can make yourself

vulnerable to another person, they will begin to feel an attachment to you, and they will take everything that you tell them more seriously.

Play to your strengths

In developing a personality that you can wear outwardly to influence people, you need to start playing to your strengths. One of the reasons why Steve Jobs was great at influencing people was not only because he knew how people worked, but because he was both intelligent and passionate. Not to mention, intense. All of these, when put together, create a very potent mixture used to influence other people.

Unfortunately, chances are likely that you are not Steve Jobs nor can you come close to being as good as he was. As a result, you really need to know how to play to your own strengths and recognize what parts of your personality have the most influencing power.

For example, if you're a smart person, but you aren't very well-spoken, focus on saying more with less. You're naturally good at working with abstract concepts, so go ahead and figure out ways to orchestrate these concepts and bring people over to your side. Use your intelligence as your foundation in your influencing. Don't, however, make the mistake of coming off as though you're trying to sound intelligent. Don't, for example, abuse a thesaurus or anything like that. This will ultimately lead to people not taking you seriously, and they may even put you beneath them.

If you're well-spoken but not very practically intelligent, stay away from the finer details and focus on using your charisma to bring people over. If you can't connect dots, don't try to. Don't bring up the dots that don't even exist, so that the person on the other end of the conversation can't connect them for you and prove your plan wrong. If you absolutely must mention them, then mention them in passing and quickly move forward to another topic. Preferably one that you can say more about and will engage the other person so that they will skip the small details in what you were saying before.

In general, just know the things about you that people will find generally appealing and then try your best to actually work within those confines.

Avoid condescension

If you want to influence people, then this is pretty important. You should never be condescending towards another person, nor do you want to say something that will explicitly make them feel terrible. This is negative manipulation, and it comes with the inevitability of bringing harm. You can consider using these sorts of tactics as a kind of collateral damage. You should treat your end goal like a jewel heist. Ultimately, you're doing it for yourself, but try to get out of there without hurting too many people.

Condescension is specifically one of the biggest ways to turn people away from your cause.

Be charming

We've already talked about this a bit in the chapters prior. It's incredibly important that you are charming, and that you can fit into any situation. It's hard to define a certain charm, but essentially it all boils down to practicing the things that we talked about in the last chapter so that you can develop your own sort of charisma.

It is this charisma that you will charm people with. Note that charming doesn't necessarily mean that you're trying to seduce or engage other people. What 'charming' means in this context is that there is a manner in the way that you speak that easily draws people to what you're saying. Charm, after all, isn't necessarily a sexual or attractive concept. It's just the ability to pull people in.

While this might seem like a little simplistic in terms of a suggestion, there really is no way around it. You need to build a superficial sort of charm for yourself so that you can easily pull people into what you're saying. It's completely and totally necessary. So while there isn't a lot to say here really, it needed to be mentioned as an essential part of your manipulative skills.

Making the impossible possible

This somewhat refers to the concept of overselling. However, one big thing that you want people to do is something that's impossible. If you can sufficiently get them on board and excited with the passion that you emanate, the idea of making something impossible possible will very much keep them involved with the project or idea at large. While things may be a little bit outlandish, with enough passion, you can keep them involved and push them further than they would normally push themselves.

You can bundle this with the idea of making them feel essential to a given mission. If you make them feel like they're the only people who can make this happen, then they're more likely to go along with it. Just be careful not to make them feel too much pressure, as this can exhaust all of their enthusiasm.

Speaking of which...

How to get the flakes

The fact of the matter is that a lot of people have an innate sort of 'expiration date' for an idea. For example, if it's some sort of joint venture that you talked them into, if you really build it up or oversell it and you give them enough time before jumping into it, they're going to start poking holes in the idea itself. Once this happens, you can consider your partnership as good as over. They'll start giving up on it entirely.

What you can do instead is be wary of this expiration date and then use the tactics listed prior to getting them to start working on it. The sooner that they start working on it and the more that they invest themselves, the sooner the 'sunk cost fallacy' starts to set in and the sooner they will start to feel an attachment to the idea itself.

The expiration date on an idea differs from every person as well as the gravity of the idea. Usually, this is one of those things you can feel out after a few interactions with a person, but you don't always have that long before you need to influence somebody. Do bear in mind, though, that you can take advantage of these concepts to get those people who otherwise have the tendency to overthink and get out of their commitments.

Know your contrarians

It seems like a really basic idea to introduce the concept of reverse psychology in this book, but the fact is that some people are just going to do the exact opposite of what you tell them. So what do you do in these cases?

Contrarians are an interesting breed to influence. Unfortunately, you don't always know they're contrarians until you first really try to work with them and get them to do something. Sometimes, though, you do have the good fortune of observing them ahead of time and see how they're likely to act.

So what do you do if you're trying to work with a contrarian? The best thing to do is not to try pushing them but to veer them hard towards the opposite of what you want. Contrarians are typically very defiant and will meet a certain amount of vigor with an equal amount of opposition.

There are, however, also scared contrarians. These are contrarians who always talk themselves out of anything that anybody else tells them. In these cases, you need to slowly push them towards the opposite of the thing that you want. They will likely follow along until the last second, at which point they'll pull the reverse all at once.

Working with contrarians can be mildly frustrating, but they're not terribly difficult to figure out once you have a keen idea on how you should go about handling them. They don't even need much practice because the same techniques apply, your position just changed.

Strike people off-guard

It almost feels redundant to say this at this point, but it's of the utmost importance that you try to catch people off-guard. Whatever they're expecting, try to do the exact opposite of it. Not all the time, of course, but you're trying to make yourself look good, different, and trustworthy. In essence, you're trying to do what you can to make yourself look like you are somebody who can influence them.

One way to catch people off-guard is to maintain complete eye contact when you're telling them about something you genuinely care about or want to make it seem like you genuinely care about it. Use your intuition here, of course. Don't come off as creepy in the name of being influential. However, the right eye contact adds a degree of intensity and dominance to the conversation that's unparalleled, and if you practice it enough, you can easily make people come around to whatever you want them to do in tandem with the other things on this list.

Make them feel special

This is one of the most important things in this whole lesson. If you take nothing else to heart, just remember this: your goal is to make the other person feel like they're essential to whatever it is that you're doing.

Don't misunderstand though. People know when you're trying to flatter them or butter them up. You can't just give them obvious compliments and expect them to be gung-ho about your project or idea. If anything, they may feel like you're patronizing them, and this will turn them off from accepting your idea.

Rather, you have to make them feel like they have unique skills that nobody else does, or like there's some specific reason that you're coming to them for help. Make them feel needed. If you can do this, then there's a pretty good chance that you can get them to agree with your ideas.

Recognize everything as a variable

This is a more general tip, but if you're trying to get to things in a very clear-cut manner like going from point A to point B, you need to recognize that everything has a variable you can manipulate. If your influence extends far enough, you aren't solely restricted to getting what you want out of one person. You can engineer entire situations based on the influence you've developed with people so that you can actually have the entire situation go in a certain way rather than having it rely on just one person.

If you decide that you'd like to do things this way, do bear in mind that you're basically going against the current in a lot of ways. You need to set your plan up so that everything has a fallback and that if any single element falls through, the plan either stops and doesn't go any further or the plan can continue without that step. This is because ultimately your situation is contingent upon variables that aren't necessarily supposed to be used, or that aren't supposed to be used in a 'true' manner. This means that the things in your situation have a higher chance of going wrong than going right. This doesn't mean your plan is doomed, it just means that you need to have a series of fallbacks in place because of the possibility that something might not work. Remember that you're actively engineering a situation here. Everything in this situation is your own doing and is based on the influence and variables that you set up. Don't place too much confidence in that unless you're absolutely certain everything will go over smoothly.

Chapter 7: Language and Psychology — Words to Make People Tick

In this chapter, we're going to discuss neuro-linguistic programming and how it applies to everything else we've covered in this book.

Believe it or not, we've already covered a few certain neuro-linguistic programming concepts. Several things in the last chapter had to do with the idea of neuro-linguistic programming under the hood.

What exactly is neuro-linguistic programming? We've made it this far into the book but haven't given it an exact definition just yet. Neuro-linguistic programming is the idea that you can use language to insert ideas into people's minds basically. In other words, you're subtly making suggestions that will eventually be accepted by a person's subconscious.

Through these techniques, you can slowly get people to accept whatever it is that you want them to do. Over a long period of time, people will come to see you as a primary influence, if you'd like to be. You can use the favors that you garnered with people to ask them for favors in turn.

Some of the ways that we've been using neuro-linguistic programming so far are setting up unique paradigms of honesty and outwardly charming personality traits. The combination of your general charm and your unique manner of speaking to people will make them see you as a trustworthy person.

Another way that we've discussed it is in the notion of taking yourself out of the equation and then framing the argument towards the thing that you want under the pretense of being objective. When you do this, you set things up such that the person starts to see you as impartial and objective. This is important because it programs people to value your opinion above the opinions of others because they see it as a more 'sound' idea than what others can offer.

So in the end, how can you take advantage of the concepts of neuro-linguistic programming to build your influence among people? There are a couple of different methods.

The first and foremost is to use it to establish an emotional connection between groups of people and yourself, or just one person and yourself. You need to start using terms like 'we' rather than 'I' to set up a subtle deference to either you or the group and a quiet sense of responsibility towards either you or the group. Don't completely replace 'I,' but do start referring to you and the person or people in question as a unit. This is an important part.

The second is to make yourself seem enigmatic. You do this by throwing people off-guard and coming off as someone who is very unique, as I've said before. Your goal isn't to ostracize or weird people out, though, so don't take it too far. What you ultimately want is for people to describe you positively, and that they see your personality and way of handling things as fundamentally distinct.

There are some other ways to use language to subtly turn people against things or in favor of things. These work best either from a false-objective standpoint (like the detached standpoint that we talked about before) or from a position where they see you as an influential person. There's actually a deep connotation with positive and negative words, such that even using positive or negative words in relation to something when somebody cares about your opinion can create a situation where they innately start to connect those positive or negative words to those concepts. For example, if you were trying to present one college as good and one college as bad, you could use vaguely good terms and phrasing to define the first while using vaguely bad terms and phrasing to define the second.

If you're too overt in this approach, people will realize that you're trying to make a contrast or a comparison between the two subjects. Rather, you need to use subtle phrasing. The first college, for example, may be 'affordable,' 'have great programs,' or 'a solid foundation.' The second college may be 'out of the way' or 'a little plain,' or you may just be 'a little worried about how good a degree from this one will look.'

It's with the use of these subtle phrases that you can begin to slowly program somebody's opinions regarding certain topics. Enough of this over time, and you can start to dramatically shift somebody's opinion on something.

Another way that you can program someone's opinions is to actually overstep the thing you don't like. For example, if you were trying to make an argument against something, you could say something so erroneously good about the opposition that the person will start to see it as ironic in their own mind and slowly see through what you presented. This is a very subtle and difficult thing to pull off, but it can be very rewarding when you do it right.

Remember, words have great power. One of the most important things that you can do is learn how to use this power to bend things in your favor.

Chapter 8: Understanding Breaking Points

This chapter will break from the previous chapters because, at this point in the book, we're going to start being a bit more cautionary than we have up to this point. That is, we're going to start discussing some of the drawbacks of these methods and how to avoid them.

As I said earlier in the book, your end goals should be treated like jewel heists. You enter, you get what you need, and you leave without trying to hurt people.

It's because of this that it's important that you understand the nature of 'breaking points,' as well as how to recover from them if you find one.

Even within the context of negative manipulation, which rests outside the slow method of neuro-linguistic programming, there are certain boundaries that you simply can't cross or else your entire plan might fall through.

So what is a breaking point in the context of manipulation? A breaking point comes down to essentially what you can say or do to a person before they either start to see through you or before you've done something absolutely irredeemable.

A breaking point would, for example, is taking advantage of somebody's traumatic life experience for your own benefit. Remember that you're trying to get people to do what you want them to, you're not trying to break the people. If this sort of situation ever comes up, avoid taking direct advantage of their experience and instead wait it out so that they have time to recover before you try making use of them again.

You'll understand breaking points more with experience, but they're an important topic that you should start thinking about, so I've decided to cover them briefly. Always be wary of a person's situation and the strain that you're putting on them emotionally because too much can cause everything to fall apart, for both you and them.

Chapter 9: The Art of Lying

In this chapter, we're going to discuss a concept that a lot of people seem to overthink, lying.

Let's face it, if you want to tap into people's psyche, you need to lie at one point or another. Lying is an art, there are good liars and bad liars. Some people are so good you'd never even know they were lying despite using polygraph tests or putting them under psychological scrutiny until you see the truth right in front of you, and you finally realize that there was something off with what they were saying.

Lying is important to manipulating people. There are a lot of mistakes that people make when trying to learn how to lie 'properly.' We're going to cover what lets a person know that you're lying so that you can avoid any of those pitfalls.

The first and most obvious pitfall is the renowned

'web of lies.' Getting caught in a web of lies is terribly embarrassing, but it's easier than you think. If you tell a lie, make sure you make careful note of exactly what you're saying, so that you can come back to it later. If you feel that you need to lie, think about it ahead of time so that you can poke any holes in it and patch them up before your 'audition.'

This leads naturally into the second biggest issue, something that a lot of people do when they try to lie is to make it sound like it was rehearsed. If you ever listen to somebody speaking naturally, it doesn't flow perfectly as if they were reading from a script. In fact, it tends to flow rather awkwardly, even among the most well-spoken people. This is because the brain and the rest of you tend to become essentially detached when you're speaking off the cuff. It takes a second to think, process, and then say your thoughts. If you have a long train of thoughts, this becomes even more difficult. Sound as natural as you possibly can. Practice your lie and your intonations and be sure that they sound like your genuine voice. You know the saying, "It takes a long time to look like you just woke up?" The same applies here, it takes a lot of rehearsal to sound unrehearsed.

Another thing that a lot of people do is that they use excessive or insufficient body language. For example, a lot of people know that old gem of knowledge that people who are lying will touch their face or avoid eye contact or look up at the sky. Because of this, they'll start to overcompensate with extremely awkward facial and head language. For example, somebody who is trying to seem like they aren't lying will often make too much eye contact. While it's worse to avoid eye contact, doing too much can be quite bad in and of itself. Be careful not to go overboard in the pursuit of telling a lie.

Lying, ultimately, is not very difficult. There is a methodology to it. The first thing that you need to do is think ahead of your lie, if possible. When you have the time to consider all of the possibilities that stem from the lie, you can start to revise your lie before you ever need it. This makes it less likely that you've got a paper-thin lie.

When it comes to lying, you need to relax. Do whatever you can to relax, in fact. Take deep breaths before you need to lie, think about something else, do whatever you can to get your mind off of your lie. Or, more importantly, take your mind off the fact that you're lying. You might even spend some time before you lie trying to convince yourself the lie actually happened, that way it comes out as truth. Of course, your subconscious mind will know that the lie didn't happen, but if you can have your conscious thought processes acting as though it did, that should be enough to at least clear through the lie.

One of the things you must never do if your lie starts being questioned is to get defensive. Defensiveness is the number one reason that people get caught for their lies. Regardless, getting defensive over a lie will make people trust you a lot less than they would otherwise. The best thing to do if your lie is questioned is to stick to your guns but do so in a rational way. Explain yourself further, but you need to be careful that you don't explain too much. If you have to give more than 2 sentences after being questioned just to explain yourself, you've messed up critically somewhere.

The real trick is to just think of yourself as though you were telling the truth. If you were telling the truth and asked to defend yourself, what would you do? You would still tell only the truth. Let's say, for example, that your boss asked you if you finished a report. You actually had, and you put it on his desk. So, you say "Yes sir, I put it on your desk," and he says "No, it's not there. Did you finish it?"

What would you say? What you wouldn't say is something like "Yes sir, I was up all night working on it, and I put a huge amount of work into it. It's a great presentation, and I have no clue why it isn't there. Do you think that maybe somebody else has it? Or the cleaning lady picked it up by accident?"

You'd say something along the lines of "Yes sir, I put it on your desk, I'm not sure why it's not there. Could somebody have gotten ahold of it?" That's all the explaining that you would actually do. Don't put pressure on yourself to do anything more when you're lying. It becomes terribly transparent.

When the lie is finished, you, unfortunately, will have to keep track of it. This is one of the most difficult parts of lying in general. You'll have to maintain the lie for the duration of time that the lie will directly affect anybody. You may genuinely want to consider keeping an encrypted lie journal on your computer if you intend to lie often or have a particularly hairy lie that could easily get out of hand.

In the end, though, lying is relatively simple. It's an important part of your repertoire if you want to influence people. Lying is like manipulation, it isn't inherently bad as long as it doesn't hurt anybody. While you can definitely consider it as taking advantage of people, as long as nobody is getting hurt then that isn't an explicitly bad thing. Morality is ultimately very vague, and the ends will often justify the means. This is no exception.

Chapter 10: "I See Myself in You" — The Importance of Identification

In this chapter, we're going to discuss the importance of one key concept: getting people to identify with you. This is one of the key aspects of neuro-linguistic programming concepts that we need to cover in this book in terms of manipulation. There's a lot to be said about getting people to identify with you. It's a necessary skill, and it is one of the most important seeds that you can plant in somebody's mind.

What does identification mean? Identification refers to somebody's ability to reflect themselves in a given person. Identification can go both ways, but the second that you identify with someone, they will automatically think of you in a more positive light.

It's ingrained in the human psyche to seek social validation. When you say that you see yourself in somebody, you either see them as a version of you, or you see yourself as a version of them. You are validating that person's desire to be validated. They'll become more sympathetic to whatever you have to say because they'll start to see themselves as an extension of you.

This is something you have to do after knowing a person for a bit though and establishing some sort of rapport and common ground with them. You can't just say this right off the bat, or else it will come off as very contrived.

So what kind of situations can set you up to drop this bomb on them? Consider doing so if you need to influence a decision of theirs one way or another. If they've already established respect for you and you're in a position of seniority to them, you can say that you see yourself in them and then explain why. Provided that you haven't misread their respect for you, they'll take it as a compliment. This can be how you can turn a follower into a worshipper, in one sense or another. Validate their respect for you, and they'll start being more accepting of anything you say.

What if it works the other way? Let's say that you have somebody above you and you're trying to take advantage of their power for your own personal gain. How can you go about doing such a thing? By flipping it around, of course.

The difference is that in this context, you don't want to drop it before asking for something, it will come off as just flattery, and that will make them more likely to deny your request altogether. What you can do instead is drop it in casual conversation like this example: "I see a lot of you in myself, sir, I think you've rubbed off on me."

This will plant a seed that will start to fester over time, making them identify more with you. You'll have validated their desire for respect, and in return, they'll start to respect you as well. They will likely not defer to you, but it does give you wiggle room to ask for something or exercise your influence, provided you keep working and garnering more favor with them.

All in all, this is one of the more important lessons in this book because it's a concept that perfectly expresses the goal of neuro-linguistic programming in manipulation and influence which is to say something that makes people start thinking the way that you want them to. They'll never even know what your end goal is, they'll just see you as how you painted yourself, as an extension of them.

Chapter 11: Navigating the Psyche — Predicting Reactions

In this chapter, we're going to discuss one of the more difficult topics to really understand what's going on in a person's head well enough to predict their reaction to whatever it is that you might do. Sadly, this isn't as straightforward as one might like it to be.

A lot of predicting people's reactions comes through a combination of experience and through reading them, especially through the things that we discussed in the psychoanalysis chapter. Predicting reactions is, undeniably, one of the hardest aspects of effectively manipulating people.

Fortunately, since the methodology for neuro-linguistic programming moves a little bit slower than it does for other manipulation techniques, you don't run as huge of a risk in trying to get something out of somebody, because you generally don't use neuro-linguistic programming techniques to get something in the short term. Rather, you use them to get something in the long-term, as well as to build the rapport necessary to get things in the short-term.

Neuro-linguistic programming in this manner can then be seen as a manner of building influence as well as subtly implanting things in people's psyches to get them to accept certain topics over a long period of time.

In other words, the necessity of predicting people's reactions shouldn't be too great because you should have already built the influence that you need to have them react the way that you want them to react. However, there are still some uses for it.

Generally, you want to try to exert your influence when people are in a positive mood. If somebody is in a negative mood, you can take advantage of that negative mood in certain circumstances —

especially if they're the kind of person who runs on anger or spite — but for the most part, the best position for working with people is when they're in a mood that could be considered somewhat positive.

Do note that when you ask something from somebody, it's almost always will make their mood lean a little bit more towards the negative side. This is just how it goes. Everybody, regardless of who they are, feels like they're being taken advantage of a little bit when somebody legitimately asks something of them. This is why much of this book's notes on a conversation where you're trying to exert influence comes down to simply trying to overcome the fact that they're going to be put off, so you can place yourself in a position where you can easily override their opinions.

For the most part, you should have some idea of how people will react to something based on how they act towards you. It's important, though, that you make sure you get the clues. Don't overextend yourself. It's very easy to make requests that are altogether a poor decision. Don't try to make one huge demand. Instead, you should try to make a series of small demands over time. This is how you truly get a lot done while exerting your influence.

Getting people to do small things will generally play out favorably without giving away that you're actively trying to manipulate them. The chances are far greater that someone will go along with you to complete a small task that only they can help with as opposed to something that has a generally large impact.

Chapter 12: What to Do If You're Discovered — Regaining Favor

So let's say the worst has happened. You've been caught out in a lie or, worse, somebody has realized that you're trying to actively manipulate them. What can you do in this situation? How do you get back into a position where the person can trust you?

Well, from here, there are two possibilities. The first is that the bridge will be burned entirely from their end. In that case, there's not a lot that you can do to redeem it, unfortunately. Even if they still talk to you, they will in one sense or another be completely shut off to any sort of emotional connection with you. The only possible way around this is if they catch you in a moment of true vulnerability at a later point and then start to come around on you again, but even then the process will be terribly slow-going to the point that it's hard to really say if it would be worth it.

Now, let's consider the other possibilities: they're gullible, or the transgression wasn't bad enough that they'd try to burn bridges with you at least. In this case, there's a procedure that you should likely follow. You can tailor it to whatever situation has popped up, but in general, the best method probably is to follow a relatively similar approach.

The first thing that you need to do is accept all the blame they will throw at you. Don't send it back at them, this will only start to make them dislike you. In these cases, you really just need to soak up whatever they do.

Then, give it a few days before you talk again to this person. Depending on how close you two were and how serious the offense was, you may need more than a few weeks or a few months. However, chances are good that for most small conflicts, a little less than a week will be an appropriate amount of time to wait.

After your self-imposed exile, you need to try talking to them. By that, we mean, genuinely talking to them. Don't try to reach out to them through email or text, because the chances are likely that they won't respond. However, a short email expressing your interest is much more useful instead of speaking to them face-to-face.

Really, both techniques have their own respective perks. If you speak to them face-to-face and you're good at showing whatever emotion you want to show, you can easily convince them that you're genuinely sorry for what you've done. If you keep the interaction relatively brief and then sheepishly walk away, you can make it come off as though you actually feel bad about what happened.

On the other hand, the email presents a lot less of an initial obstacle for them to overcome. While they may not respond at all, this may be what you need; an email gives them the opportunity to respond when they feel they should respond if they feel they should respond. It doesn't put them on the spot as a face-to-face confrontation would.

Really, which one would work best will depend upon your specific circumstances. However, most of the time, the first one will be your best option.

Let's assume that you proceed with the first option. What do you do after you apologize? The thing to do afterward is to give it a few more days to let the apology sink in. If they accept your apology and they seem genuine about it (use the emotional reading skills we've developed to tell!), then try to set up a drinking session with them and some mutual friends. This can be a great opportunity for the two of you to have a 'moment of truth' where you confess how badly you feel about what happened. Be sure there are other people there, though, so that no bad blood occurs between the two of you, especially if they're a rowdy drunk and may still be harboring some anger. Here, though, you can finally bury the hatchet and hopefully go back to being good friends. I'd recommend after this that you not manipulate the person any longer, as you really only get one chance to patch things up with people when you manipulate them. They don't fall for it a second time.

If they accepted your apology but didn't seem genuine about it, your best course of action is to wait a bit longer and then start some discourse with them that's unrelated to anything professional or academic. Don't, for example, find a reason to ask them about the test that's coming up. Do send them something that reminded you of them, though. Maybe even just send them a message out of the blue that says, "Hey, how are you?" It's not very intimidating and gives them the freedom to respond whenever, but it also shows that you're serious about rekindling the friendship that you had with this person.

If they strictly don't accept your apology, then it's alright. They will either come around and see themselves as the jerk for not accepting your apology when you were being genuine about it (If you came across as being genuine about it, that is. They may reject it because you're clearly being fake), or they may leave the bridge burned, never to be fixed. The first is a far better position to be in than the second, so hope for the second.

All in all, it's not too difficult to get back to square one from wherever you are. Really, it's just a matter of knowing who you're working with and the exact situation that you're in. I'd like to say one more time that you really shouldn't be putting yourself in situations where you're negatively manipulating someone. If you're just using people as thoroughfares and treating them like people in the meantime, then you shouldn't really have any huge issues aside from being caught in a lie, especially if you're being smart about your tactics.

Conclusion

Thank you for making it through to the end of *NLP*, let's hope that it was informative and that the book provided you with all of the tools you need to achieve your goals whatever it may be.

The next step is to start using all of this information so that you can move people in the directions you want them to go. These skills are valuable, though often unspoken because they're in a moral gray area. Therefore, it's up to you whether you do the right or wrong thing with them. If you practice these techniques, there's a good chance that you'll end up getting whatever it is you're wanting.

Thank you!

Before you go, I just wanted to say thank you for purchasing my book.

You could have picked from dozens of other books on the same topic but you took a chance and chose this one.

So, a HUGE thanks to you for getting this book and for reading all the way to the end.

Now I wanted to ask you for a small favor. **Could you please take just a few minutes to leave a review for this book?**

This feedback will help me continue to write the type of books that will help you get the results you want. So if you enjoyed it, please let me know!

www.ingramcontent.com/pod-product-compliance
Lightning Source LLC
Chambersburg PA
CBHW052103110526
44591CB00013B/2326